HISTORIC NEW CASTLE NEIGHBORHOODS

North Jefferson and North Mercer Hill Houses

Susan Urbanek Linville

Historic New Castle Neighborhoods: North Jefferson & Mercer Street Hill published February 2013 by Susan U. Linville

Cover design by Susan U. Linville

Text and unattributed photos copyright of Susan U. Linville

ISBN: 978-1482353877

Photographs marked "lchs" are used with permission from the Lawrence County Historical Society. For use or reproduction contact the society at:

Lawrence County Historical Society

PO Box 1745

408 North Jefferson Street

New Castle, PA 16103-1745

Email: lawchs@verizon.com   Phone: 724-658-4022

ACKNOWLEDGEMENTS

I would like to thank Anna Mary Mooney, Betty DiRisio, Lynn Slovonsky, Andrew Henley and Steve Ramey for their comments and assistance in making this book possible.

A Short History

The New Castle area was originally occupied by the Delaware tribe. When John C. Stewart arrived with his brothers in 1798 and erected his log cabin, rattlesnakes were plentiful and gray wolves common.

Other settlers followed and purchased "donation lands" near the confluence of Shenango River and Neshannock Creek. One of those settlers was Crawford White. He purchased lot No. 1953, which includes the area occupied by North Jefferson and North Mercer Streets.

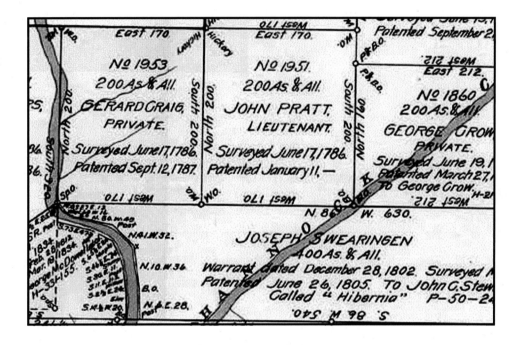

The Erie Canal Extension came to New Castle in 1833. Because of the availability of transportation and ready access to raw material markets, business flourished. Numerous manufacturing plants became located in New Castle including iron and tin plating companies. The canal system was later supplemented and then replaced by the Pittsburgh and Lake Erie Railroad, which offered greater speed and capacity. New Castle's population swelled from 611 in 1840 to 28,339 in 1900, and to 38,280 in 1910, as immigrants flocked to the city to work in the mills and nearby limestone quarries.

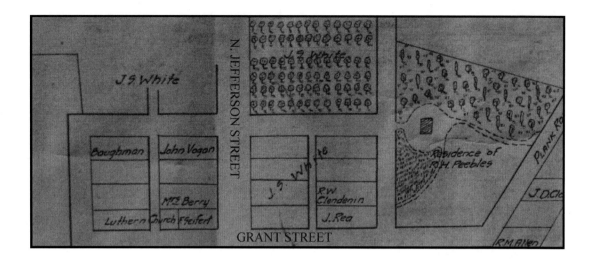

1855 Map Tracing

This neighborhood was first home to Crawford White. He built a log cabin on the east side of Jefferson Street just up the hill from Grant Street. A farm house was later constructed north of a "deep ravine" at the top of the hill beyond the Wilmington Road-Jefferson Street split. Crawford White died in 1834, leaving property to his sons, James D. White and Joseph S. White. Over time, plots were sold, as can be seen on the 1855 map tracing above. In 1872 (see map below), after the death of James, Joseph S. White still owned a great deal of the land along Jefferson Street Hill, including a house on the west side of Jefferson Street, north of Grant Street. Joseph moved to the farm in the 1880s and continued to sell property on the hill.

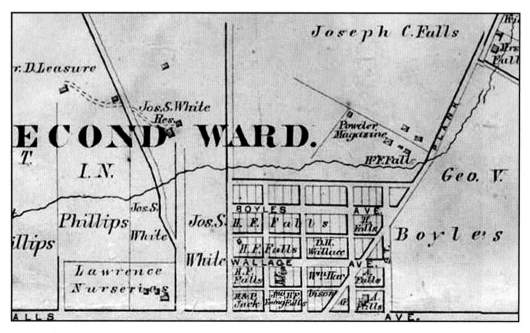

1872 Map

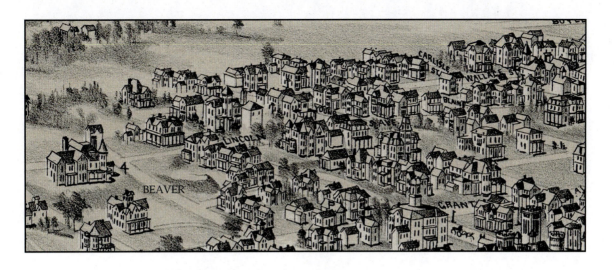

1896 Drawing of Neighborhood

New Castle's Historic District

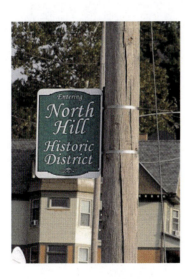

New Castle's North Hill Historic District was entered into the *National Register of Historic Places* in 1999. The 91-block district consists of roughly 450 acres of land that sit slightly north of New Castle's business district. The area is historic due to the many ornate homes and mansions that lie within its boundaries. The district includes many fine examples of Italianate, Queen Anne, American Foursquare, Bungalow/Craftsman, Victorian, Romanesque Revival, Gothic Revival, and Neo-Classical homes.

This neighborhood booklet includes homes dating as far back as 1859 that were built by merchants, bankers and industrialists.

Mary Davidson

11 EAST WALLACE AVENUE
Style: Gable Front Suburban Built: 1890s

Mary A. Pettit Davidson

Mary A. Pettit was one of eleven children born to Nathaniel and Barbara Grieb Pettit, on their farm where Elwood City stands now. She graduated from Edinboro Normal School in 1866 and married Robert James Davidson in in 1868. They lived on his family homestead two miles south of Wampum. He "fitted himself by private study for a teacher," taught for ten years in the local school district, was a Republican and member of the board of school directors, functioning both as secretary and president. Mary also taught at New Castle High School under Professor W. N. Aiken.

Robert was known for his retiring manners and sound judgment. When he died, Mary moved with her daughter Eva and son William Fred to Beaver for four years, California for a year, and then moved to Wallace Avenue in New Castle in 1898.

Mary was active in the community. A member of the Methodist Episcopal Church, she worked as president of the Foreign Missionary Society. She was also named president of the Almira Home executive board and member of the building committee. Almira Home was founded in 1893. Under the encouragement of Mrs. Ella J. Reeder of Edinboro, Mrs. Almira P. Martin led several women on a door to door campaign to seek funds to open a facility for aged women. On August 18, 1893, the official charter was drawn up.

The original Almira Home (left) and new building (right).

Mary was also active in the Women's Christian Temperance Union, whose Crusaders formed in 1873 and held their first organizational meeting in Chautauqua, NY, in 1874. She taught Sunday schools, several normal classes and the Mary A. Davidson Bible Class. When she died in 1918 she was remembered as one of the "most strenuous workers for the public good."

17 EAST WALLACE AVENUE
Style: Colonial Revival Built: late 1870s

J.J Montgomery

Montgomery House

Land on the northwest corner of Wallace and Mercer was deeded in 1877 from Joseph S. White to J.J. Montgomery. Montgomery was a merchant who sold grain, seeds, flour, feed, hay, cement and fertilizer. The house was the home to Montgomery's family, including his younger son, Charles, until he married wife, Caroline, and moved to 251 Mercer Street. After Caroline's untimely death in 1895, Charles moved back to Wallace Avenue with his daughter Ella to live with his mother. Charles was a cashier at the National Bank of Lawrence County and a member of the Central Presbyterian Church. He later remarried; his second wife, Margaret, was listed as a widow in the 1917 directory.

National Bank of Lawrence County

Joseph and Laura Norton

Laura Reeves was born in Warren, OH, in 1841 and moved to New Castle with her mother and sister in the 1860s. She married Joseph W. Norton in 1867. He was a harness manufacturer who worked at the Wire Nail Mill in the 1890s. Joseph died young, leaving Laura with six children by 1900 at the 12 E. Wallace Avenue home: Anna, a bookkeeper, Joseph, a telephone operator, Lyde, a music teacher, Helen, a school teacher, and two children still in school. Laura was a city resident for 40 years, a member of the First Methodist Church and one of the "best known and highly esteemed ladies of the city."

Walter C. Stone

Walter C. Stone was a superintendent at the S&W Steel Company. He lived with his wife Maud and daughter Marjorie at the 14 E Wallace house from 1900 until 1915, when it was sold to Martin V. Hall.

14(left) and 12 (right) EAST WALLACE AVENUE
Styles: Neoclassical, Front Gable Suburban Built: 1890s

Swogger & Leddy Home

This Victorian has lost its traditional decorative gingerbread. It was home to many over the years. John Swogger and his wife Anna moved from New Wilmington to live in the Mercer Street house with their son, Lawrence, a medical student, and their daughter, Blanche, a nurse. John was a fifty-four year old insurance agent in 1900, but didn't live out his retirement on Mercer Street.

The house was empty in 1905 and then home to several people before James Leddy and wife Ellis called it home in 1914. James was a tailor for G.W. Warner. Ellis Statts Leddy had moved to New Castle from Newark, NJ, as a child. Her father was a partner in Staats and Crawford Lumber Company.

411 NORTH MERCER STREET
Style: Gable Front Victorian Built: 1890s

409 NORTH MERCER STREET
Style: Neoclassical Built: 1890s

John C. Hart

John Hart was born in Washington, PA, in 1851, son of William and Elizabeth Oliver Hart. After attending public schools, he learned the marble cutting trade under Joseph Howarth in Washington. In 1872, he moved to New Castle, where he worked in the marble and granite Monumental business. He married Ella T. McComb in 1876 and they had four children. They were living in the Mercer Street house by 1900. He was a member of the First Christian Church and served on the board of elders. He was also a member of the No. 69 B.P.O.E. and the Woodsmen of the World.

William Stritmater

13 EAST LINCOLN AVENUE

Style: Neoclassical to Villa Built: before 1900

The Stritmater house underwent extensive renovation with the addition of brick to the exterior and tile roof (see photo below of the house before renovation)

William A. Stritmater

William Stritmater was born in 1841 in Beaver County to John and Mary Jane Stritmater. His father died in 1850, when William was only nine years old, leaving his mother to support four children. Being the oldest, William went to work early to help the family, working at R.W. Cunningham's foundry for 25 cents a day. At thirteen, he became a nail machine feeder apprentice. Being an ambitious man, at 20, he left the foundry to clerk at B.H. Henderson & R.W. Stewart's store at the corner of Mill and Washington Streets.

After fighting in the Civil War with the Fifty-fifth Volunteer Infantry, William returned to New Castle to become a partner at Henderson & Company. In 1869, he opened Stritmater Brothers, a dry goods business on Washington Street, with James R. Stritmater and W.R. Johnson. They dealt in dry goods, millinery, carpets, merchant tailoring, boots and shoes, and the building still advertises their name to this day.

In 1890, William lived on Pittsburgh Street with wife Elizabeth E., their daughter, and 3 servants. He was widowed and living in the Lincoln Avenue house by 1900, and married Elizabeth Gaston in 1903 at the age of 61. He was considered a "dean in the merchandising business in the city," was prominent in the United Presbyterian Church, and worked up until three weeks before his death in 1921.

Then & Now

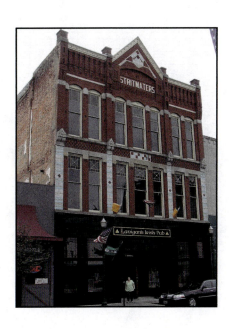

George Warner

George Warner worked as a tailor for Pearson Brothers until joining with Thomas Daryman in 1893 to open his own business, Daryman & Warner, located on N. Mercer Street. He lived on Wallace Avenue until he married Anna B. Brown in 1896 in the Evangelical Church. After the wedding, the young couple "set up housekeeping" in this Mercer Street Victorian that still has its original slate roof.

414 N MERCER STREET
Style: Winged Folk Victorian Built: 1890s

327 NORTH MERCER STREET
Style: Neoclassical   Built: 1870s

Charles Watson

1872 drawing from Mercer St. House on right. Owner unknown.

Kells-Watson House

Susan Mills Kells, was born in Ireland and widowed in Steubenville, OH, when her husband, George Kells, died in 1860, leaving her with two daughters. She lived with her mother-in-law for the next twenty years, not moving to New Castle until 1882. Her reason for moving is unclear, but Hannah Raney was from a prominent family in Steubenville and may have encouraged Susan to move to the house adjacent to her own. Susan's older daughter, Sallie, married James McConahy. Younger daughter, Georgianna, married Charles Watson at the residence in 1886. They were married by Rev. J. D. Herron of Trinity Episcopal Church. The wedding was attended by Leander Raney and his wife and other neighbors. Charles was part owner of Brown, Thompson and Co. with Wm. Brown, A.W. Thompson, C. E. Mengie and J. McKee. They sold, dry goods, notions, groceries, provisions, boots, shoes and other items at their store on E. Washington Street. The Watsons lived in the house until 1910.

315 NORTH MERCER STREET
Style: Second Empire Built: 1859

Mr. and Mrs. William Patterson

William Patterson

William Patterson was born in Beaver County in 1824 to Samuel and Ester Patterson. As a student, he worked at a tannery during summers. He spent a number of years working in retail for John B. Pearson and Daniel Euwer before opening a wholesale/retail drug store in 1848. Unsatisfied with the retail business, he was instrumental in developing coal fields in the region. Between 1860 and 1900 he organized Aetna Iron Company, was half owner of Crawford Iron and Steel Company, and founded New Castle Wire Nail Company. He was involved with the Beaver Coal and Coke Company, Penn Coal Company, Beaver Valley Railroad, and Pennsylvania Engineering Works. He was also a prominent banker, opening Patterson Bank. Shenango Valley Hospital was opened in 1894 with his backing.

Carriage House on Jefferson Street

William married Anna Mills in 1852. The house was built in 1859, and its third floor ballroom undoubtedly entertained New Castle high society. One can imagine they enjoyed the luxuries of the family's wealth, such as the convenience of indoor plumbing and marble bath fixtures. Anna gave birth to two daughters and a son before her early death. Harriet Woodward became Patterson's second wife. They had three more children.

By 1911, the Pattersons no longer owned the home. The house was remodeled at some point and the central roof tower was removed (see photo below). The Carriage House, which can been seen from North Jefferson Street, was sold and became Dean & Miller Auto Repair by 1924.

Leonard M. Uber

Leonard was born in Mercer County in 1870, but didn't move to New Castle until after he graduated from Grove City College in 1893. He entered the office of Judge Norman Martin, began his study of law and was admitted to the bar in 1895. He partnered with Rufus C. McKinley in 1907 and practiced before the Supreme and Superior Courts of Pennsylvania.

Leonard did not limit his business to the practice of law. He held interests and stock in Ohio and Illinois oil fields and was director and stockholder in the Standard Wire Company and Union National Bank. He was director of the Telegraph Key Cushion Company, chartered in 1912, and incorporated the Port Huron Citizens Telephone Company in Michigan with Charles Greer and others with the "intention to install a modern telephone system."

He married Edna Crawford Young in 1900. According to the New Castle News, the "couple were prominent in New Castle social circles." Their marriage date was kept secret until the affair "leaked out." Leonard was a Democratic leader, and member of the First Presbyterian Church and thirty-second degree Mason of the Blue Lodge Chapter, Council and Commandery at New Castle.

306 NORTH MERCER STREET
Style: Colonial Built: about 1900

J. Norman Martin

302 NORTH MERCER STREET
Style: Queen Anne Victorian   Built: 1890s

Honorable J. Norman Martin

Norman was a well known member of the New Castle community and judge of the 17th District, which included Lawrence and Butler Counties. He was born in 1859 and graduated from Westminster College in 1881. After practicing law in Kansas, he moved to New Castle and joined with D. B. and L. T. Kurtz. He was admitted to the bar in 1883 and practiced law with S. L. McCracken until 1886. He married Jane Andrews in 1884 and they had one son before he became a judge in 1892.

Norman was interested in civic matters. As a member of the Common and Select Councils, he helped establish a city sewage system and was involved with street paving projects. He was also a stockholder and director of New Castle's first electric light company.

303 NORTH MERCER STREET
Style: Queen Anne Victorian   Built: 1870s

Robert W. Clendenin

Robert W. Clendenin

Robert Clendenin was born on the family farm in Cumberland County, PA and moved to New Castle in 1840 at the age of fifteen. He worked at a dry goods store, eventually starting his own business at the corner of Mercer and Washington Streets in 1848. R.W. Clendenin and Sons carried dry goods, notions, carpets, draperies, oil cloth, and other goods. An 1897 New Castle News article reported that the cellar of Robert's first residence at the rear of his store was used to house escaping slaves. He never admitted to being part of the underground railroad, but "a twinkle in Mr. Clendenin's eyes … suggested that he might not have been ignorant of what his friends were doing with his cellar."

Robert married Belinda Pollock, daughter of Dr. Joseph Pollock, in 1846 and had five children. One son, Joseph, died in infancy, and another, John, died as a teen in 1870. William joined his father in business. Daughter, Mary E., married Edward H. Ward, who was involved in iron manufacturing and died in 1903. They lived in the house with Robert and Belinda and their daughter Helen. After the deaths of Robert and Belinda, Mary Ward lived in the house until her death.

Clendenin Store

22 (left) and 18 (right) EAST GRANT STREET
Style: Queen Anne Victorians Built: about 1900

Herbert D. McGoun

Herbert D. McGoun was the born in 1868 to Harvey E. and Mary McGoun. Havrey owned H.E. McGoun & Sons, a well known boot and shoe store on Washington Street. They were known for their well stocked and large selection of boots, shoes, slippers and rubber goods. They were "always aiming to give the best for the least money; they are second to none in their business." Herbert worked at the store with brothers Ralph and Samuel. He and his wife Ida K. lived on Mill Street before moving to the 18 East Grant Street home about 1900.

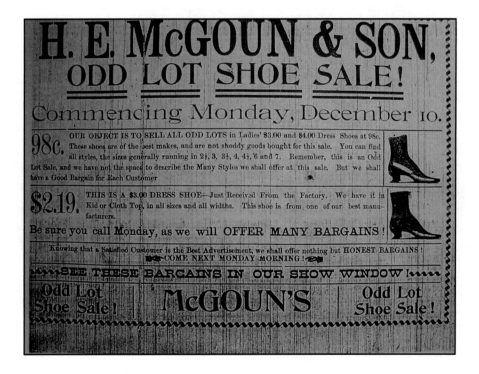

Joseph R. White

Joseph White moved to the 22 East Grant Street house about 1900 with his wife Mary McClymonds White and their adult children Florence and Charles.

306 NORTH JEFFERSON STREET
Style: Queen Anne Victorian Built: 1880s

William S. Foltz

William Foltz was the son of Samuel Foltz, a lawyer with interests in the iron industry. William followed in his father's footsteps, investing in the Greer Tin Mill in 1893 and New Castle Paint and Varnish Company in 1902. He worked with his father at Foltz Bank, organized in 1864, which consolidated with First National Bank in 1883. When Samuel died, William became president. He was also chairman of Knox, Foltz & Co., LTD. William Foltz was living in this stately Victorian in 1890.

J.P.H. Cunningham

New Castle Grocery Company

John P. H. Cunningham

By 1900, John Cunningham had moved into the house with wife, Helen, a son, his mother-in-law, Mary Howe, and two servants. John was the son of R.W. Cunningham, who moved to New Castle in 1836 and opened a business transporting wool, glass, iron and steel to the west. He later built a foundry for plows, stoves, mill gears and iron pipes, and invested in the New Castle and Beaver Railway and National Bank of Lawrence County. John began working for his father at the foundry and later operated the New Castle Grocery Company warehouse with William B. Howe.

310 (top) and 312 (bottom) NORTH JEFFERSON STREET
Style: Queen Anne Victorian Built: late 1890s

Louis N. Crawford

Louis Crawford was born in 1869, son of James and Elizabeth Crawford of Union Township. He was a prominent citizen who attended public schools before becoming involved with the steel business. He worked at New Castle Steel until it went out of business, for two years he worked at National Steel as a supervisor, and then at Carnagie Steel Company until 1907. He was director of the National Bank of Lawrence County, a member of the First Presbyterian Church, a Knights Templar Mason and member of the Lawrence Club.

Louis married Katharine Sweeny in 1894 and they were living in the 310 North Jefferson Street home by 1900.

William Withrow

William Withrow was one of the most highly esteemed residents of Mt. Jackson. He lived and worked on the family farm until the late 1880s, when he moved with his wife, Elizabeth, and his daughters to New Castle. They lived at the residence at 312 North Jefferson Street until 1902 before returning to the family farm. William died in 1907. Elizabeth followed in 1910, dying at the Shenango Valley Hospital in her 80th year.

305 NORTH JEFFERSON STREET (1850s-1956)
LOST UNDERGROUND RAILROAD LANDMARK

TODAY
Parking Lot

Thomas Berry

Mary Berry

BERRY-WHITE HOUSE

Thomas Berry, listed as the first successful barber in New Castle, lived in the house on this property prior to 1850. Thomas died in 1853, leaving his wife, Mary, with their six children, including P. Ross Berry, who was a bricklayer at the time and would become a notable builder in Youngstown, OH. The house was said to contain a secret cellar room. The Berry's involvement with the underground railroad is undocumented.

Joseph White married Adaline Pollock, daughter of Dr. Joseph Pollock, in 1841 and worked with her father at his lumber mill for several years. Joseph and Adaline originally lived on North Street and moved to the brick home between 1855-60. Their involvement with the underground railroad is highly documented. In one letter (part of the Siebert Collection) Joseph said, "We were living in the brick house near the big willow tree…," referring to the North Jefferson Street house. They had been part of the underground for quite some time, and hiding escaped slaves was taken in stride. Joseph noted, "One pleasant afternoon, the Rev. Hanna, an old side Covenanter minister then preaching in New Castle, came up to our house and said there had just come into town a wagon load of refugees, and he had come to see about making arrangements for keeping them overnight; the arrangements were easily made."

Joseph and Adaline White

Perry Maitland

311 NORTH JEFFERSON STREET
Style: Cross Gables Folk Victorian Built: 1886

Perry Maitland

When Crawford White died in 1865, he left property to his children, including Amada M. White, wife of D. Craig. The Craigs sold the 311 North Jefferson Street property to Joseph Ferver in 1870. Joseph Ferver was born on his parents' farmstead in 1817, educated and worked on the farm. He married Nancy Carle in 1847 and they had 5 children. He built a house on the property before 1872, but not the house that stands there today.

Joseph Ferver's daughter Adeline married Perry Maitland in 1871. Perry was a real estate dealer and land owner, born in 1844 to William N. Maitland and Camilla Pollock, who owned a farm north of the city. Perry worked as a clerk for W.R. Clendenin and eventually owned and operated his own grocery store. In 1874 he built a three-story block of buildings, which he later sold to the Citizens Bank, and moved his store to Mill Street. He also dealt in real estate, and was a "very heavy taxpayer," according to the county history.

In 1886, Perry built this Victorian on North Jefferson Street, where he resided until his death in1897. He and Adeline had no children to inherit the house. It was sold after Adeline's death in 1900.

Washington Street looking west toward Mill Street.

307 NORTH BEAVER STREET
Style: Neoclassical   Built: 1904

Elmer I. Phillips

Isaac N. Phillips

Original house of Isaac Phillips stood in the block behind the existing house on Beaver Street.

PHILLIPS-MOORE HOUSE

Built in 1904, this house was constructed for Elmer I. Phillips and wife Beulah Ingels Phillips. Elmer was a son of Isaiah Phillips, who owned much of the property along Beaver Street. Elmer was born and educated in New Castle. He graduated from Butler University in 1884 and practiced law in New Castle for 10 years. Elmer was also a political heavyweight, elected to City Council in 1892 and to the Pennsylvania State Senate in 1904. In addition, he was secretary and general sales agent for the Lawrence Glass Company, and a member of the board of directors for both the Lawrence Savings and Trust Company and New Castle Portland Cement Company. When the Shenango Valley Hospital was built up the hill from his house, Elmer became a trustee and treasurer.

The Phillips family lived in the house until 1914, when they moved to Highland Avenue. The house was sold to Winfield S. Moore and his wife Edna. Winfield was born in 1867 to Lawrence County pioneers John G. and Elizabeth Faurbach Moore. Before moving to the city, he lived in the Nashua district, where he allowed many of the old circuses to winter on his property. Winfield became a representative for Perma-Stone, trademarked by a Columbus, Ohio, company in 1929, and introduced the product to many in the U.S. and Canada.

William Norris

House in the 1970s

312 NORTH BEAVER STREET
Style: Gable Front Victorian Built: 1880s

William Norris

P.C. White was the original owner of this property. He sold it to Ellen Gith Baughman in 1857. She and her husband, Andrew J. Baughman, originally from Maryland, built a house on the property in the early 1860s. Andrew was a wagon maker and an assistant engineer at the Eagle Engine House Fire Department. His eldest daughter, Selena, was a seamstress by the age of fifteen.

The property and house were sold to William and Rachel Bonhan Norris in 1870. William was born near Blackburg Chapel in Allegheny County in 1836. He was originally a drayman, flatbed wagon driver. By 1880 he owned his own grocery store located on Washington Street. William and Rachel reared two sons, Edwin and John, who joined their father in the business. William Norris & Sons handled groceries, provisions, flour, feed, crockery, glass, stone and tin ware.

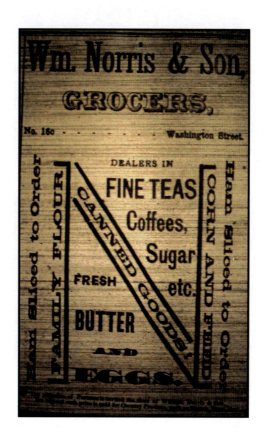

William and Rachel were upstanding members in the community. Unfortunately, in 1895, William suffered from an attack of the grip, followed by pneumonia, and died at age 59. He was a respected member of the community, member of the Methodist church and Sunday school superintendent for 25 years. It was estimated that 1,000 people attended his funeral, including fifty of his Sunday school students. Nearly every grocery store in the city was closed, with about 60 grocers attending. Rachel survived well into her 80s and still lived in the house in the 1920s.

317 NORTH JEFFERSON STREET
Style: Gable front Suburban Built: 1890s

Thomas W. Davis

Thomas Davis was born in Wales. He worked at Etna Iron Works for a time and then managed Kline Hardware Store in West Pittsburg. He and his wife, Hannah, lived in the house with their children Frank and Mollie.

William Eichbaum

William Eichbaum was born in 1844 in Allegheny City, son of William and Mary Sample Eichbaum. At fifteen, he joined the Mt. Jackson Guards, Battery B, First Light Artillery, known as Cooper's Battery. After the war, he was general manager for Clark and Company, which became Clark & Eichbaum mercantile business. He later became president of Union National Bank.

William married Clara Cooper, 20 years his junior, in 1886. They were living in the Jefferson street house by 1890, but had no children. William participated in G.A.R. encampments with his neighbor and former commander, James H. Cooper. He died in 1925 on the date on which he was mustered out of service at the close of the Civil War. Clara died a year later of pneumonia.

319 NORTH JEFFERSON STREET
Style: Colonial Revival Built: 1880s

321 NORTH JEFFERSON STREET
Style: Queen Anne Victorian Built: late 1890s

James H. Cooper

lchs

Captain James Harvey Cooper

Captain James H. Cooper was an honored and respected member of the community at the turn of the 19th century. Called modest and retiring by General Meade, he was a veteran of the Civil War who participated in more than twenty-seven engagements.

Cooper joined the Mt. Jackson Guards in 1861, and the company was accepted as part of "Battery B" of the First Regiment of the Pennsylvania Light Artillery. He quickly rose through the ranks to become captain and led his men through battles at Antietam, Fredericksburg, Gettysburg and Petersburg.

During the battle of Antietam, "Captain Cooper had a very narrow escape. While directing the fire of the guns on Poffenbuger's farm, on the morning of the 17th a solid shot struck his horse and tore it in pieces," according to author Samuel P. Bates. The regiment played a key role at Gettysburg repulsing Pickett's charge. Thirty-eight were killed and fifty-two seriously wounded.

After the war, Cooper lived with his wife, Alice, at 321 North Jefferson Street. He partnered with Benjamin Butler and opened their store on Washington Street. They were listed in the directory as clothiers, hatters and furnishers. He was first stricken with sickness at a G.A.R. encampment in 1905 and died the following year.

Cooper on the battlefield

Cooper second from left

330 NORTH JEFFERSON STREET
Style: Queen Anne Victorian Built: 1890

Leander Raney   David Jameson

RANEY-JAMESON MANSION
"The Castle"

Raney's first home on Mercer Street

Leander Raney was the son of James, owner of five grist mills in Lawrence County and Ohio, and Sarah Raney. Sarah purchased a lot on Mercer Street, directly behind the mansion, in 1867. The family lived in a house built there until after Leander married Hannah Mahon from Steubenville, OH, and they moved to the mansion in 1890. Leander and his cousin James Raney owned Raney Milling Company in Mahoningtown, where they produced "as fine a quality of flour as is made anywhere" under the White Lily brand. He also owned Raney & Burger Iron Works.

In 1911, the house was purchased by David Jameson. Jameson was a well known banker and financier. He co-founded Citizens Bank, and donated $600,000 to build Jameson Memorial Hospital. He and his wife, Jessie, had two children. David Jameson Jr. met an untimely death from a head wound received during a 1926 assault. Jameson, Sr., already in poor health, died shortly thereafter. In 1929, Jessie presented the hospital to the city of New Castle and Lawrence County. When Jessie died in 1942, her daughter donated the mansion to the hospital.

The mansion was transformed into apartments for nurses until 1964, when it changed hands and became part of New Castle Business College's four-acre campus and home to Alpha Iota Sorority.

In the mid-1980s it was purchased by Fredrick Cioffi and became Castle Manor, a personal care home that housed mentally ill and mentally challenged individuals. Cioffi invested heavily in renovations and equipment. His investment had almost paid off when a tragic fire struck June 15, 1998. None of the 28 residents were injured, but two were later arrested in connection with the blaze. The third floor and roof were engulfed. The original slate roof, decorative wood on the gables, and third floor windows were lost. Water damaged some of the plaster and wood floors. The roof was replaced to prevent further damage inside, but Cioffi never did rebuild. The house is currently under renovation.

407 NORTH JEFFERSON STREET
Style: Queen Anne Victorian Built: 1890s

Dana Cooper Butler

Almira Home

Benjamin F. & Dana Cooper Butler

Benjamin F. Butler was a lifetime resident of New Castle. He was active in both civic and business affairs early in life, and was first employed as a foreman at the New Castle News. He left the newspaper in the 1890s to become a merchant with Captain Cooper and worked at the store until the 1920s when it became Reynolds and Summers Clothing Store.

In 1934, Butler was inducted as a city councilman and became head of the street department. He also served on the Board of Directors of the Lawrence Savings and Trust Company.

Butler married Dana Cooper and they moved into this fine Queen Anne Victorian on North Jefferson Street. They were members of the First Christian Church, where he was deacon and on the official board for 40 years. Mrs. Butler was active in the community, participating in the A.C.T. Class 1914 Book Club and serving on the executive committee of the Almira Home for Aged Women for 43 years.

Like all business men, Cooper and Butler were not shy about offering deals. They advertised a "great price-cutting sale" in an August 1907 issue of the New Castle News. Men's pants, normally two to five dollars, were marked down to one to two dollars. Men's and youth's odd vest sizes were selling for fifty cents each. Junior suits were an extra value. Only one dollar.

409 NORTH JEFFERSON STREET
Style: Queen Anne Victorian Built: early 1900s

Standard Brewing Company

Henry Grotefend

Henry Grotefend was born in Hanover, Germany, in 1861 and moved to New Castle in 1898. He reorganized Standard Brewery Company with George W. Lamoree and took on the position of vice president of the company. His brother Albert joined them as brewmaster. They produced 65,000 barrels per year and employed 30 workers until encountering problems during Prohibition.

In January 1923, a secret operation was undertaken to discover if Standard Brewery was selling beer with an alcohol content over 1.5 %. Agents watched a rail car being carefully loaded on a sidetrack on the company grounds. They found 239 cases from many different breweries in Pittsburgh, Aliquippa, Columbus, Fort Wayne, St. Louis and St. Joseph, MO. Suspicious, the agents confiscated the shipment and sent samples to a chemist to be tested. The beer was found to have an alcohol content greater than 5%.

Henry testified in court in March 1923 that Standard Brewing Company had made a mistake in filling the bottles. He explained that during manufacture, they brewed normal beer which was boiled off to create the lower alcohol content product. The bottles in the rail car had obviously been filled from the wrong cask. The jury did not buy his story. In May 1924, Henry and other officials were sentenced to 10 months imprisonment in the Allegheny County workhouse and fined $1,500 for violating prohibition laws.

Henry was a member of the B.P.O.E. and I.O.O.F. He and his wife, Sophie, had six children. They died with in twenty-four hours of each other in 1932. Double funeral services were conducted by Rev. Stump of St. Paul's Lutheran Church and Rev. Pearson of Trinity Episcopal Church.

Samuel Klafter

Samuel Klafter and Judy Storch Silverman

Samuel Klafter came to the United States from Austria-Hungary in 1886, arriving in Sandusky, Ohio. He established cigar stores in New Castle, Youngstown and Canton, OH by 1897, but during the Great depression, the Ohio stores were closed.

Samuel and his wife, Bertha, built their Jefferson Street House in the 1920s, but never had any children. Samuel's nephew, Morris Storch, joined his uncle in the business after returning from mandatory service to the Kaiser in WWI as an interpreter (he wasn't yet a U.S. citizen). Morris' daughter, Judy, married Lee Silverman, and they continued on with the business. In 1993, Randy Silverman became the fourth generation in the family. Klafter's now operates three core businesses out of its New Castle office: wholesale candy and tobacco, Smoker Friendly/Cigar Express stores, and premium cigar mail order.

411 NORTH JEFFERSON STREET
Style: Colonial Revival   Built: 1920s

Original Store

413 NORTH JEFFERSON STREET
Style: Colonial Revival Built: early 1900s

Horace A. Rugh

Horace Rugh was born in Greensburg, PA, in 1855 to Dr. Jacob Welty and Rebecca Gilcrist Rugh. In 1871, he moved west and worked on a cattle ranch for several years. He married Emma Osborn in 1887 and they moved to New Castle in 1900. Horace bought the old Teser Ice Plant on West Grant Street. Under his management, the newly named Lawrence Ice and Storage Company made ice from distilled water. They had the capacity of several tons daily and employed 15 men by 1906. Ground was broken in 1913 to build a new addition and double the capacity of the plant. The Rughs had three children and Horace lived at the house until his death in 1930.

Lawrence Ice and Storage Company

503 NORTH JEFFERSON STREET
Style: Colonial Revival Built: about 1900

Charles Matthews

Charles Matthews attended school until he was about fourteen years of age, working in the mills in the summer and going to school in winter. At the age of sixteen years, he was apprenticed to the trade of roll-turner in the iron mills, and at nineteen attended business college. In November, 1894, he became business manager and treasurer of the Lawrence Guardian, and continued in that position after the Guardian was consolidated with the Courant. Afterward, he engaged in banking and manufacturing.

He married Miss Elizabeth Lutton, daughter of William B. and Jane Lutton in 1888, and they had three children. They lived on Court Street until 1900, when they moved to the house on North Jefferson Street. They were active members of the Presbyterian Church and popular in the community.

Charles was a prominent Mason, and had taken high orders, belonging to the following organizations: Mahoning Lodge No. 243, F. & A. M., of which he is past master; Delta Chapter, No. 170, R. A. M., of which he is past high priest and trustee; Hiram Council, of which he was T. I. G. M.; Lawrence Commandery, No. 62, Knights Templar, of which he was past eminent commander. He was grand steward in the Grand Lodge of Pennsylvania in 1895-96.

Charles was a member of the city council from 1887 to 1893, and sheriff of Lawrence County 1897 to 1900. While a member of the select council he served as chairman of the finance and fire committees and was a member of other important committees.

He was a delegate to the Republican State convention in 1886, and elected to the 62nd Congress, but was an unsuccessful candidate for reelection in 1912. He was appointed county commissioner of Lawrence County on November 26, 1924, and served until January 2, 1928.

After a full life of as a private entrepreneur and public servant, he died peacefully at his home on Jefferson Street in 1932.

62nd Congress in Session.

406 N. JEFFERSON STREET
Style: Colonial Revival Built: 1904-05

George Greer

Alice White Greer seated at right.

Original House

GREER-CLAVELLI MANSION

George Greer, son of William Greer, was an important player in the manufacturing and industrial development of New Castle. He was vice president of First National Bank, director of National Bank of Lawrence County and an original stockholder in the Shenango Valley Steel Company. In 1892, he organized the New Castle Steel and Tin Plate Company and was president and manager until it was absorbed by US Steel Corporation. When the Shenango and New Castle Works were purchased by American Tin Plate Company, Greer became manager. New Castle was the largest manufacturer of tinplate in the world. George was associated with several other manufactures in the area.

George married Alice White, daughter of Joseph S. White, farmer and landowner. Joseph sold land along North Jefferson Street to Alice and George Greer individually and they built their first house on the property in the late 1870s. The existing house, designed by Frank Foulke, was built in 1904-1905. The Greers lived in the house until their deaths in the 1920s. Their daughter, Amanda Greer Love, occupied the house until 1965 when it was sold to Joseph A. Clavelli. He set about restoring the house and donated it to the Lawrence County Historical Society in 1982.

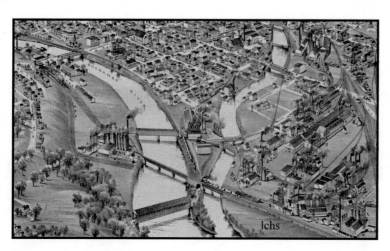

New Castle Manufacturing along the river
Fowler 1896

Charles Greer

lchs

414 N. JEFFERSON STREET
Style: Unclassified Built: about 1899

Charles Greer

With his brother George, Charles Greer was one of the first manufacturers of tinplate in America. He worked as a bookkeeper and then assistant manager at the Tin Mill.

Charles married Grace Greenwood Marquis in 1897. Grace was the daughter of Captain Milton S. Marquis from Mahoningtown. Milton was a canal boat owner with a fleet of fourteen boats who settled in New Castle area in 1855. He was involved with coal, limestone and brick manufacturing, and later established the Home Trust Company in the city.

Charles lived in the house until his death in 1925. Grace followed in 1937.

Shenango Tin Mill

REFERENCE & PHOTO SOURCES

Atlas of the County of Lawrence and the State of Pennsylvania, G.M. Hopkins & Co., Philadelphia. 1872

20th Century of New Castle and Lawrence County Pennsylvania and Representative Citizens. Ed. Hon. Aaron L. Hazen. Richmond-Arnold Publishing Company, Chicago, IL 1908

Biographical Sketches of Leading Citizens. Lawrence County Pennsylvania. Biographical Publishing Company, Buffalo, N.Y. 1897

History of Lawrence County Pennsylvania. Compiled by Wick W. Wood. 1887

U.S. Census: 1850-1920

New Castle City Directories: 1890-1960 (New Castle Public Library and Lawrence County Historical Society)

Photographs and Lawrence County Deed Books. Lawrence County Historical Society, PO Box 1745, 408 N. Jefferson St., New Castle, PA 16103

New Castle Public Library Microfilm Newspaper Collection: New Castle News, New Castle Courant, New Castle Democrat, New Castle Weekly, Lawrence Guardian, & Lawrence Journal

Library of Congress, 101 Independence Ave SE Washington, DC 20559

Online resources:
Archive.org
Familysearch.org
Genealogytrails.com
Lawrencecomemoirs.com
Fold3.com

Made in the USA
Monee, IL
06 July 2023

38111799R00036